Teaching Your Child

To Read

for the FUN of it

written and illustrated
by

Patricia C. Beall

Hand in Hand Publishing
East Glenville, New York

Library of Congress Catalog Card Number: 88-82067

ISBN 0-9621138-0-8

Printed in the United States of America

for

Danny

Your enthusiasm for life is like a contagious disease that I'm so glad I've caught. Thank you, my son.

Table Of Contents

Introduction

Although this is a book concerned with teaching a child how to read, its main purpose is not an academic one. Rather, its purpose has been to devise a method by which parents and their children can procure maximum enjoyment of each other's company, before the beginning of school.

If you are a parent searching for ways to spend time with your little one, let me suggest to you several advantages of using reading as a tool to this end. First of all, reading has no age limit. It is a skill that the parent, himself, enjoys daily and therefore, is an ideal solution for the parent who is uncomfortable in his four year old's world. Secondly, children who are ready to read progress rapidly. Their self-confidence abounds. To be the initiator of this growth is a source of continual pleasure. In addition, there is no fear that the child will enter into a situation that is too mature for him, because his evergrowing vocabulary will only give him access to those books written especially for his age group and interests. Last of all, teaching a child to read before school begins is unnecessary; therefore, a *no-pressure* situation is created where both parent and child can relax and read because they want to, not because they have to.

If your child completes this course, he will have a reading vocabulary of over four-hundred words. He will be able to discover new words on his own by sounding them out. If your child spoke previously in incomplete sentences, you will find that he expresses himself more maturely.

The course encompasses twenty stories and poems. Preceding each story is a vocabulary list of twenty to twenty-five words. These words will permit your child to read the succeeding story, and they will be used repeatedly throughout the course. You will find short notes above each vocabulary list informing you of compound words, plurals and other material that you will need to be aware of. Midway through the course is a chapter of suggestions for expanding your child's learning experiences. Further suggestions are discussed in the concluding chapter.

You should be aware that the vocabulary was chosen with the interests of four and five year olds in mind, with an emphasis on their feelings and observations and consequently, will be most beneficial to this age group. Because proper names change dramatically from generation to generation, I have chosen to ignore them and focus on general relationship terms, such as: mom, dad, sister, brother, grandma, grandpa, etc. After an initial background of personal pronouns, verbs and prepositions, the nouns have been employed to create the scenes. Whether the story centers around a trip to the ocean, an illness, a trip to a city or outside in the yard, common words have been chosen enabling your child to identify with the experiences presented.

The only prerequisite to this course is an exposure to upper and lower case letters of the alphabet. If your child is familiar with the alphabet, but not necessarily an expert, he is ready to begin. As you and your child spell out each new vocabulary word, you will find that he acquires a working knowledge of the alphabet very quickly.

The materials you will need for this method of teaching are index cards, a black finepoint marker and a 6x9 inch pad of unlined paper. If these materials are unavailable to you, feel free to improvise.

By this time you will have observed the use of the masculine gender in all references to your child. The purpose of this usage is, not to neglect the female portion of our population but rather, to maintain the rhythmic flow of each sentence- he instead of he/she, him instead of the choppy him/her- facilitating your rapid understanding of all instructions.

Chapter One

Getting Started

Let me begin by assuring you that your child will be reading long before he completes this list of twenty-five words. This method of teaching involves the introduction of words which are immediately utilized to create full sentences. The possibility of writing a sentence exists from the moment your child learns his first two words. It is imperative to always write complete sentences. For example, do not write, "boy finds girl," rather write, "The boy finds the girl." If you want your child to speak intelligently, write intelligent sentences for him to read.

Initially, I suggest that you only introduce two words per day to your child. Eventually, increase this amount to four words or more as you observe the growth of your child's ability and self-confidence.

In this course, the most important word for your child to learn is his own first name. He will not read his name in any of the stories, but you can use it to manufacture interesting, even comical, sentences for him to read. For instance, which sentence do you think your child would enjoy more- "The cat drinks milk from his bowl" or "Danny drinks his milk from the cat's bowl"? Appealing to your child's funny bone is the quickest way to teach him.

You now have enough background information to begin the course. First, take your pad of paper and turn it so that its width is greater than its length. If your child can not recognize his own name, print his name in the upper left-hand corner of your pad. This corner is reserved for the two vocabulary words of the day and should be boxed in after you have introduced those words. Proper names must begin with capitals. Print all other words in legible lower case letters. Now, take one word at a time. Tell your child

think
under

My baby is under my feet.
Do you think that you can learn to read?
This toad thinks he can hide from us under the ground.
What do [...] family picture
under th[...]

prepositions
in at of on about out under into up by from around to

nouns
tree lot family cat toad worm dog bird jar rug hand bag around bee time day house table

verbs
think pricked hop flies walk hit drop come has fly bite pick does put
can sit read run take will see learn was let do go eat like
be want play hide find lost look is

what the word is. Then have him repeat the word after you. Ask him if he can tell you what the letters of the word are. If he needs help with any of the letters, offer help. Make sure that he is aware of any capital letters. Read the word again by slowly sounding out each letter while pointing to it. Now introduce the second word similarly.

When both words have been discussed, the rest of the paper can be used for writing sentences. There is space for a minimum of six sentences. The order in which you choose to teach the primary vocabulary list will determine how soon sentences can be formed. By the time your child knows five words, you should be able to write some. Your child will probably begin by reading each word as a separate entity. It is important for you to demonstrate how words can flow together to express a thought or idea, by repeating each sentence after your child.

It is time we consider plural endings to words. Each vocabulary word in this book has *s, es* or *ies* typed in parenthesis next to it. This is its plural ending. *S* and *es* are tacked onto the end of a word to pluralize it. Words with *ies* require you to drop the *y* and add *ies*. Suppose you have taught your child the three words: *the, boy* and *eat*. You want to manufacture a sentence using those words, but it sounds like, "The boy eat." Place an *s* on the word *eat*. Now your sentence flows- "The boy eats." When your child reads the pluralized word, cover the *s* and then reveal it at the appropriate time with its accompanying sound. This is not a difficult concept for your child to grasp, especially if you enthusiastically hiss like a snake. I suggest that you refrain from using *ies* endings until the second half of the book.

Recognition of the two printing styles of the lower case letter *a* must be taught. School age children learn to print the letter a like this-*a* . However, a majority of printed material contains this letter *a.* Your child must be able to use both *a* s interchangeably. Give him one week to adjust to your teaching method; and then, introduce the alternate letter *a* by twice printing a word that contains *a*, explaining that the *a* s can be printed either way, but the word, itself, remains the same. You should consistently vary your use of the letter *a* in composing sentences until you realize that your child has mastered this concept.

Not only is it important to recognize the difference in

printed *a* s, it is, also, imperative to identify a word, regardless of whether it is capitalized or not. Beginning each sentence with a capital letter will aid to this recognition process.

Last of all, teach your child how punctuation is employed, thus insuring that his reading is never a flavorless monotone. When sentences end with a question mark, demonstrate the manner in which his voice should change pitch. Exclamations are exciting, breathless sentences. Italicized or underlined words are to be emphasized. Reading will interest both of you more if you read dramatically.

The supplemental requirement of this course is the use of flash cards. Each new word is printed with a black finepoint marker on the unlined side of an index card. Words containing the letter *a* should be printed on both sides of the index card. The index cards are flipped through daily as reminders of previous lessons. When you conclude teaching a set of vocabulary words, place a rubber band around them. Children tend to rebel against reading too many flash cards, so I suggest that you show your child no more than one set daily.

You will notice that each vocabulary list is divided into groups of verbs, nouns, prepositions, etc. This arrangement is to assist you in preparing a set of approximately seven index cards on which you can print all known words to date, permitting you to remember them for use in sentence structuring throughout the course. All verbs should be on one card, nouns on another and so on.

I want you to realize that your gentle persistance may be necessary while your child is learning his first forty-five words. This is a time of insecurity when your child can doubt his own abilities. However, there will be no stopping him once his self-confidence emerges.

Checklist

A. **INTRODUCE TWO WORDS** (one at a time) by placing them into a box in the upper left-hand corner of your pad.

   1. **IDENTIFY THE WORD** and have your child repeat it after you.

   2. **IDENTIFY ALL LETTERS** of the word.

   3. **SOUND OUT** each letter as you read the word again.

B. **CREATE SENTENCES** that begin with a capital letter.

C. **DON'T FORGET *S* AND *A*.**

D. **USE FLASHCARDS.**

Vocabulary note:

You are looking at a primitive story. It contains twenty-five words, many of which seem insignificant. To your child, however, no word is inessential, since this is his initial exposure to all of them.

The pluralized words in this story are *want, hide, look, find* and *eat*. There are, also, three questions. *The, she* and *where* are words whose first two letters combine to create new sounds. Teach your child to recognize *th, sh* and *wh* combinations and their unique sound when introducing these words.

If your child is a slow reader, remember to repeat every sentence of the story after him to illustrate the flow of each idea. He will learn, by your example, to read faster but more importantly, to comprehend the essence of all he reads.

Vocabulary #1:

the	boy(s)	want(s)	to	and	house(s)	him	where	mad
	girl(s)	play(s)	with		table(s)			
	he	hide(s)	for					
	she	find(s)	in					
		lost	at					
		look(s)						
		is						
		go(es)						
		eat(s)						

The boy wants to play with the girl.

He wants to hide, and the girl wants to find him.

The boy hides.

The girl looks for the boy.

Where is the boy?

Is he lost?

The girl looks and looks and looks.

She is mad.

She wants to go in the house to eat.

The girl finds the lost boy.

Where is he?

He eats at the table in the house.

Chapter Two

The Next Twenty

Vocabulary note:

In this story twenty new words are introduced and used in conjunction with the primary vocabulary list. You will notice that sentence length has increased as we attempt to develop your child's comprehension skills.

Like, sit, read, run, picture, house, tree and *bike* are all pluralized. Don't forget the combination sound *wh* in the word *while*. You may need to explain the meaning of the word *while* to your child. If so, tell him that it means *at the same time*, and use examples like- " You eat your breakfast, while I do the dishes. You eat your breakfast at the same time that I do the dishes." Sometimes, *while* will represent a short period of time-"In a while,..." Remember the word *on* is in italics! The word *read* can be pronounced *reed* or *red*. Make sure to familiarize your child with both pronunciations.

Vocabulary #2:

a	baby(ies)	like(s)	of	while	book(s)	here	my
	me	sit(s)	on		picture(s)		
	mom	read(s)			tree(s)		
	us	run(s)			bike(s)		
	we						
	dad						

My baby likes me.

She sits with me while mom
reads a book to us.

We like the pictures in the book.

We see pictures of houses, trees
and bikes, like my bike.

Baby wants to play.

We hide and mom finds us.

Mom wants us to eat.

We eat at the table.

We sit *on* the table, and mom
is mad at us.

Here is dad.

Baby runs to him.

She looks at dad.

My baby wants dad to go and find a book to read to us.

Dad sits at the table with baby and me.

He looks at the pictures and reads while we eat.

Chapter Three

Reading Poetry

Vocabulary note:

Rhythmic poetry is like a spoken song. Perhaps that is why it is so appealing to children. To demonstrate this sing-song quality, begin by reading the whole poem to your child, rather than reading sentence by sentence.

The three new plurals in this poem are *lots, takes* and *learns*. You will find two questions and the *th* combination in the word *that*. Also, note the exclamation.

Vocabulary #3:

you	take(s)	about	lot(s)	sunny
that	will		time(s)	new
	see(s)		day(s)	red
	learn(s)		fun	your
	was		family(ies)	high
	let(s)			
	do(es)			

Do you want to take a look

at the pictures in my book?

Lots of pictures you will see

of mom and dad and baby and
me.

Here my mom takes time to play

with baby and me on a sunny day.

My dad reads a book to me

while we sit high in a tree.

Here my baby learns to run.

Boy, was that a lot of fun!

And here is a picture you will like.

The girl is me, on my new, red bike.

Do you want to let me see

a book about your family?

Chapter Four

A Girl and Her Dog

Vocabulary note:

In this story we meet our first animal- the dog. Since animals greatly interest children, many animals will fill the succeeding pages.

The pluralized words are *walk*, *see*, *come*, *bite*, *drop*, *hit*, *hand* and *play*. *What* begins with the combination letters *wh*. Last of all, note that the third sentence is an exclamation.

Vocabulary #4:

what	walk(s)	around	dog(s)	her	not	good
it	hit(s)	from	bird(s)		away	
	drop(s)	into	hand(s)			
	come(s)		ground			
	has					
	fly(ies)					
	bite(s)					

A girl walks her dog around her house.

She sees a bird fly away to a tree to hide from the dog.

What a day!

It is a good day to play on her bike.

The dog comes with her.

He runs around and around the bike and bites it.

The bike drops to the ground.

The girl hits the ground with her hands.

It is not good.

The girl is mad at her dog.

She takes the dog into the house.

The dog has to learn to sit while the girl plays with her bike.

Chapter Five

A Jar Of Worms

Vocabulary note:

This is the longest story to date where each sentence builds toward a specific conclusion. To test your child's comprehension, allow him to read the entire story without interruption. Then, question him to determine how much of the story was understood. Up to this point, the story format has consisted of one sentence per line. Now, however, your child will be reading paragraphs.

Picks, hops, birds, toads and *worms* are the plurals. There are four questions and an exclamation. The three words: *this, there* and *three*, contain the combination letters *th*.

Vocabulary #5:

this	pick(s)	up	feet	his	there	one
	does	out	mouth(s)			two
	put(s)		cat(s)			three
	hop(s)		toad(s)			
	flies		garden(s)			
			worm(s)			
			jar(s)			

23

We put three worms into a jar for mom to look at. Mom does not like to look at worms. She put the jar of worms out of the house into her garden.

We see a toad in mom's garden. Toads like to eat worms. We pick the three worms out of the jar. We put the worms at the toad's feet. He does not like worms on his feet. The toad hops away.

Here is the cat. Does she want to play with the worms? The cat looks at us and runs away. This is not fun! We want to see the cat play with the worms.

There is a bird that flies up into that tree. Will the bird eat the worms? We put the three worms on the ground and go hide around the tree. The bird drops to the ground. She picks up one worm with her mouth and flies up into the tree. The bird comes to take two worms this time. We see three worms go into that tree with the bird. Will she eat the worms? We look at the tree to see the bird. What is it? She has three baby birds to eat the worms for her.

Chapter Six

Two Selections For The Work Of One

Vocabulary note:

With this set of vocabulary words, you will discover not only a story but a poem as well. The poem was written to appeal to your child's devilish nature. Imagine that you are a little boy who has just been petitioned by his mother to entertain a little girl visitor, and you don't care for little girls. This is that little boy's poetic invitation to play.

The *outside in the yard* theme is concluded with these selections. From now on, your child will be reading animal fantasy stories, stories dealing with relationships, special occasion stories and those concerned with the ordinary routine of home and school.

Bug, rug, beetle, ant and *put* are pluralized. The poem contains many italicized words which must be emphasized to achieve the intended effect. Note the word *chair* with its combination sound *ch*. Also, the *th* combination sound is in the word *think*. Exclamation points are frequently used in the story, as well as a few questions.

Vocabulary #6:

I						
be	under	if	bug(s)	chair(s)	small
pricked	by		rug(s)	beetle(s)	brown
can	inside		yard(s)	ant(s)	only
think(s)			sting(s)	rain(s)	
			bee(s)		

27

In my house you will find

lots of small, brown bugs,

if you look under the rugs.

In my yard you will be

pricked by the sting of a bee,

if you go up in my tree.

Come inside and I will pick

a chair where you can sit.

Beetles and ants hide in it.

Come on out of the rain.

I think that you will see

the *only* bug here is me.

The boy walks in his yard. His dog runs around his feet. His cat runs to a tree. She sees a bird. The cat wants to eat the bird.

Hop. Hop. What is it? It is a toad on the ground. The cat sees the toad hop. She wants to eat the toad. The cat picks up the toad with her mouth. The toad is not good to eat, and the cat drops the toad from her mouth.

The boy walks to the garden. He hits the ground with his hand. One, two, three! A worm comes up from the ground. He does not like the boy to hit his house.

The boy likes bugs. He has a jar to put bugs in. There is a beetle and ants. There is a fly. A lot of bugs for his jar! What is this bug? It is a bee. The bee wants to sting the boy. The boy's dog sees the bee. He bites at it, and it flies away. What a good dog!

The boy puts out his hand. A drop of

rain hits his hand. Come on, dog! Come on, cat! It is time to go into the house.

Chapter Seven

Animal Fantasy Begins

Vocabulary note:

What could be more unlikely than a friendship between a mouse and a toad? Yet, in children's literature, stranger companions than these have been written about, attesting to the flexibility of young minds. The mouse, in this story, embodies the protective, maternal instinct found in so many children, thus enabling them to empathize with her and the toad.

Your child has learned the words *day* and *time* which are combined into the compound word *daytime*. When he is reading the story for the first time, cover the latter half of the compound word as he begins to read it, and then cover the preceding half as he concludes reading the word. Say the whole word to demonstrate how two known words can combine to form a new word. The latest plurals are *stairs, boys, sleeps, wakes, thinks* and *gets*. The combination sounds of *th* and *wh* are evident in the words *they* and *when*.

Vocabulary #7:

they	hurry(ies)	but	mouse	when	happy
	get(s)		home(s)	so	safe
	sleep(s)		stair(s)	never	all
	hear(s)		friend(s)	now	
	wake(s)		bed(s)	back	

One small mouse has a home under the stairs. That mouse is so happy. She likes to eat what the family drops from the table. It is good, but she is in a hurry to get back to her home. She wants to be safe from the family's cat.

The mouse never sleeps in the daytime. The family's two boys run in and out of the house all day on the stairs. The mouse can hear the boys and wakes up. Now she sleeps when they go to bed.

On this day, the mouse finds a new friend. A toad sits under a boy's chair at the table. The toad is lost. He can not find the yard. The mouse likes the toad and takes him to her home. The toad will be safe in the mouse's home.

The mouse wants to look for flies for the toad to eat. The toad is happy to eat the flies when the mouse comes back. In a while, the mouse can find only a beetle for the toad to eat. The toad has to get out to the yard. There will be bugs in the yard for him to eat.

The mouse thinks. The boys can take the toad to the yard. The toad sits on the stairs. The boys will come. They do not see the toad when they come. The boys will walk on him if he does not hurry away. He hops into the mouse's home where it is safe.

The mouse thinks that the boys' mom will let the toad out in the yard. The toad sits on the stairs. The boys' mom comes by. She sees the toad and gets a book to hit him. The toad hops back to his friend. He thinks he will never get to the yard.

Here comes the boys' dad. The mouse wants the toad to hurry and sit on the stairs. The toad does not want to, but he will do it for his friend. The toad sits on the stairs. The boys' dad sees the toad and picks him up. He likes toads. He puts the toad in the yard where it is safe, and the mouse is happy.

Chapter Eight

More Animals and Poetry

Vocabulary note:

To establish the rhythm of this poem, you can direct your child to pause slightly, not only at each comma, but also at the end of each line. If he does not read the poem rhythmically, read it to him to demonstrate how it should sound.

New plurals are *beds* and *chairs*. The *th* combination is found in the word *then*. Note the exclamation and question.

Vocabulary #8:

said	as	log(s)	then	sad
gone	or	nap(s)		furry
told		bone(s)		soft
bit		box(es)		
don't		hat(s)		
goes		tail(s)		
		head(s)		
		meal(s)		

" There is a mouse in the house,"
said the cat to the dog.
But the dog can not hear
when he sleeps like a log.

When he wakes from his nap
and looks for his bone,
that dog is so sad
for his bone is all gone.

"Where can my bone be?"
said the dog to the cat.
"There is a mouse in the house,
and I told you that!"

They look under the table
and in all the chairs,
under the rugs,
in the beds, up the stairs.

Then, when they think that
they never will find it,

they see a small box,
and the bone is inside it.

A furry, brown mouse
sleeps in a soft hat.
He wakes up in a hurry
when pricked by the cat.

"Run, run," said the dog
as he bit the cat's tail.
"If you don't hurry now,
you will be the cat's meal."

The mouse runs away
where it's safe from the cat
and will never go back
to that box or that hat.

And the dog is happy
when the cat goes home.
Now, he sleeps on his rug
with his head on his bone.

Chapter Nine

Grandma's Surprise Box

Vocabulary note:

Two important relationships are introduced in this story, that of a child to his sister and to his grandmother. Your child will also become acquainted with a variety of school words preparing him to read any books you discover that describe his forthcoming kindergarten experiences.

Thing, give, pen, book and *word* are pluralized. When you teach your child the word *write*, explain to him that *w* and *r* combined will sound like *r*. *Things* contains the combination letters *th*. The compound word *schoolhouse* resides in the text. There is an exclamation, also.

Vocabulary #9:

grandma(s)	left	after	room(s)	our
sister(s)	give(s)		surprise(s)	some
	open(s)		thing(s)	
	make(s)		pen(s)	
	write(s)		paper(s)	
	are		school(s)	
			teacher(s)	
			name(s)	
			word(s)	

Grandma has gone home. She left a box in her room by the bed. The box is a surprise for my sister and me. Grandma likes to give us fun things to do. Mom said that she will let us open the box after we make our beds. So my sister and I hurry.

I find that I can not open the box. My sister has to open it. She takes some things out of the box and gives the things to me. There are pens, paper and school books to read. Now we can play school.

We make grandma's room into our schoolhouse. The box is our table, and my sister is the teacher. I learn to write my name with a pen. We open one of the books, and my sister reads it to me. I can read some of the book. After that, I make lots of pictures to give to grandma when she comes back to see us. I write my name on the back of the pictures.

41

Grandma is so good to us. I want to surprise her. I can think of a good surprise. I will learn a lot of new words so that I can read a book to her. That will make grandma happy! And I like to make grandma happy.

Chapter Ten

Visiting Nursery School

Vocabulary note:

This story will acquaint your child with twins, if he is not already familiar with them. Succeeding this list of words, he will be able to recognize the terms *sister* and *brother*. Why not teach him the names of his siblings now, if he has any, for the purpose of creating a greater variety of humorous sentences for him to read.

The compound words *schoolroom, schoolwork* and *playground* are in the text. Remember to cover, first, the latter half of the compound word and then, the beginning portion, to facilitate the learning of this word. You will find eleven new plurals: *twins, makes, pants, wears, names, coats, toys, blocks, tells, days* and *girls. Sh* and *th* combinations are in the words *shirt* and *than.*

Vocabulary #10:

brother(s)	wear(s)	shirt(s)	than	same
twin(s)	forget(s)	pant(s)		different
	hang(s)	coat(s)		big
	build(s)	toy(s)		
	draw(s)	block(s)		
	tell(s)	story(ies)		
	work(s)	song(s)		

I look like my brother, and he looks like me. We are twins. Some twins look different but not us.

My brother and I go to the same school. Mom makes me wear a different shirt and different pants than my brother wears. Now our teacher will not forget our names.

When we get to school, we hang up our coats. Then, we can play with all the toys. My twin brother and I like to build block houses with the big, red blocks in our schoolroom.

The teacher wants us to sit at a table and draw pictures to take home to our mom and dad. After that, we sit around her chair while she tells us a story and we learn a new song.

On good days, we get to go out

and play. My brother and I like to run all around the playground.

School is lots of fun. It is where my brother and I learn to play with small boys and girls, like us. Some day we will go to the big school,and our teacher will not let us play. We will do lots and lots of schoolwork. Then, if there is time, we will play.

Chapter Eleven

Fun and Games With Words, Sentences and Sounds

Vocabulary #11:

brush(es)	teeth	ready
wash(es)	hair(s)	
drink(s)	boot(s)	
kiss(es)	shoe(s)	
	clothes	
	sock(s)	
	bathroom(s)	
	outside	
	breakfast(s)	
	egg(s)	
	toast	
	juice(s)	
	milk(s)	
	hug(s)	

Congratulations! You have reached the midpoint of this course. The preceding vocabulary list is not accompanied by a story or poem in an attempt to add variety to the learning method. Are you aware of how many small commands you give your child each day? For example, before you are ready to take him outside, you probably say something like this- " Brush your teeth. Brush your hair. Go to the bathroom. Wash your hands. Put on your socks. Put on your shoes. Don't forget your coat! Now, are you ready to go outside?" You have just expressed eight requests. And how

many times have you been on your way out the door to spend hours where there is no bathroom and had your child tell you that he forgot to use yours? With this latest list, you will be able to write all your requests on a piece of paper, hand it to your child and let him check off each item as he accomplishes it. In writing notes, work becomes a game, and reading is constantly reinforced.

Notice that there are two compound words in the list: *bathroom* and *breakfast*. Although your child can not recognize the two components of each compound word, you can demonstrate how each word can be split into two new words and form sentences employing them. For example, a sentence using the components of the compound word *bathroom* could be- "After you take your *bath*, go into your *room* to put on your pants." The compound word *breakfast* can be split to create the sentence-" If you hand me the box that *fast*, you will make me *break* the eggs!" It is not necessary to have both components of a compound word in the same sentence.

Your child has mastered a sufficient quantity of words enabling you to invent your own compound words. *Handsome, hatbox, catnap* and *underground* are some examples.

The *sh* combination letters are found in the word *shoe*. Up to this point, the combination letters *ch, sh, th, wh* and *wr* have been introduced. If you think that your child needs practice in this area, you can make a set of five index cards, one for each letter combination. Utilizing them as flashcards, play an acting game with him. Encourage him to pretend that he is a train as he recognizes the *ch* card and adapts its sound to his actions. The *sh* card should be associated with an exaggerated pretense- "Shhh. The baby is sleeping." Squeezing the air out of an imaginary balloon appropriately represents the sound of the *th* card. Now, have the baby wake up crying, "Waaa," for your *wh* card. And the last card, *wr*, can be represented by the roar of a lion.

Another game can be played with your store of over two-hundred flashcards. In this game, your child has the opportunity to invent his own sentences. You will need to make twenty extra flashcards, ten *a* s and ten *the* s, with a different color marker, in order to be able to extract them later, with ease, from the pile. Thoroughly mix all the cards, and pass out six of them to each player. Players' cards lie face up on the table while the residue are placed face down in a pile between the players. At each player's turn, he must examine his cards to see if he can create a *complete* sentence. Plural endings may be added to or withdrawn from any word. If the player can make a sentence, he reads it aloud to all other players, places his sentence to one side and draws replacement cards from the center pile until the total number of cards before him on the table equals six, excluding those of his sentence. If the player is unable to invent a sentence, he must draw a card from either the center pile or the discard pile and then discard one of his seven cards before the end of his turn. Although there may be times when a player can use his drawn card to complete a sentence that he is working on, he must wait until his next turn to do so. At that time, he will begin by reading his sentence and then, drawing his replacement cards. The winner of the game is the first one to create four complete sentences.

Have you taken your child to the library yet? If not, this would be an appropriate time to start. Look for beginner or easy readers. In some books, you will find vocabulary lists. Others are part of a series of books that guide children through different reading levels. Peruse each book to determine its compatability with your child's own reading level. Your child does not need to know every word in the stories that you choose for him. The weeks that you have spent sounding out each vocabulary word will allow him to identify almost all of the words that he encounters. You can supply the identity of the remaining words for him.

Chapter Twelve

What Do You Think?

Vocabulary note:

This story concludes with a question that is directed toward your child. Hopefully, the response to this question will be an understanding smile. Should your child's response be contrary to what you expect, guide him back through the story, asking him to describe what occurred and what his feelings would be if he were served an egg with shells in it and black toast.

The pluralized words are *ask, napkin, fork, spoon, move, let, bit, brush, cup* and *drink*. Combination letters *sh* are found in the word *shell*. Note the word *knives* with its combination letters *kn*. When introducing this word, be sure to instruct your child to always pronounce *kn* as *n*. Don't forget the three exclamations!

Vocabulary #12:

ask(s)	birthday(s)	behind	nice
help(s)	napkin(s)		black
set(s)	fork(s)		more
have	knives		
climb(s)	spoon(s)		
move(s)	cup(s)		
pull(s)	bowl(s)		
break(s)	shell(s)		

Dad asks me and my big sister to help him make breakfast. It is mom's birthday. The meal will be a surprise for her. Dad tells me to set the table. I get out napkins, forks, knives and spoons. What a nice table I have set! I have to climb on a chair to get the cups for our juice. My sister moves the knives and spoons behind my back. That makes me mad, and I pull her hair. Dad tells my sister to put the knives and spoons back.

My sister will make the breakfast, but dad lets me break open the egg into a bowl. I see small bits of shell in the egg. My sister does not want to take the shell out. She will make the egg with the shell in it.

Dad tells us to hurry. We have to make the toast. We hear mom get out of bed. Dad goes up the stairs to see mom. He will give us time to make the toast. We forget the toast while we put the juice in the cups. The toast is black.

We hear mom on the stairs. My sister

brushes the black from the toast with her hand. We hurry and put the egg and toast on the table. Mom walks into the room. Boy, is she happy! What a nice surprise! Mom sits down and bites her toast. She drinks a lot of juice with her toast. Mom's juice is gone. She eats her egg. Mom asks us to hurry and get her some more juice. I can tell that she likes our birthday breakfast. I think mom wants us to make all her meals on her birthday. Don't you think so?

Chapter Thirteen

Pepper and Cats

Vocabulary note:

What did you discover about your child's comprehension as you listened to his responses to the preceding story? His understanding will be challenged by yet another question at the conclusion of this story. The slightly humorous content will insure that the lack of comprehension, if present, is not due to boredom.

The plurals are *potatoes, knows, cats, smells, jumps* and *sneezes*. Combination letters: *kn, ch, th* and *wh*, are found in the words: *know, chicken, them* and *white*. Note the two questions in the text.

Vocabulary #13:

grandpa cook(s) down dinner(s) them always white
know(s) over meat(s) again
smell(s) potato(es)
jump(s) salad(s)
sneeze(s) chicken(s)
fish
nose(s)
pepper(s)

Grandma and grandpa ask me to have dinner with them. Grandma is a good cook. When I come over, grandma likes to cook meat and potatoes with a salad for me. She knows that we always have chicken or fish at our house. Grandma and grandpa have to put a book on my chair so that I can sit up at the table.

Grandma has three cats. The black and white one always makes me mad. When grandma's black and white cat smells our meat, she jumps up on the table. We have to tell her to get down. I do not like the cat's nose on my meat. This time I will put pepper on it. Up comes the black and white cat. I let her smell my meat. That cat sneezes and sneezes and sneezes all over our dinner. Grandma is mad at the cat. She does not know about the pepper. I will not tell her.

Grandpa tells grandma that he does not want the cat to jump on the table again. Grandma has to put that black and white cat outside. I get down to help grandma let the cat out. It makes me happy to see that cat outside. I walk back to my chair. Where is my meat? Grandma's white cat and her brown one sit under the table. They look so happy. Then the white cat sneezes and sneezes again. The brown cat sneezes with her. I think I know where my meat is. Do you?

Chapter Fourteen

Friendship

Vocabulary note:

A sometimes difficult experience, common to all children, is the making of new friends. Not only does the young girl in this story have to adjust to a family move, she must adapt herself to a friendship with a member of the opposite sex, a feat for one who dislikes boys. Conversation is enclosed in quotes. Explain to your child that quotation marks mean that someone is talking.

Animal, friend, shake and *turn* are pluralized. You will find the compound word *without* in the text. The combination letters *sh* are in the word *shake*, as well as the letters *wh* that are found in the word *why*. The initial question is repeated once. Explain that the word *close* can be pronounced two different ways, *clos* or *cloz*, and is defined as *nearly together* or *shutting something*.

Vocabulary #14:

could	before	zoo	why	close
moving	off	animal(s)		own
shake(s)		nothing		very
says		voice(s)		long
say				strange
start(s)				last
turn(s)				
sing(s)				

" Could we be friends?" I ask the new girl. She is moving into a house that is close to my own house. She shakes her head, and I ask her why not.

"I never play with boys," she says.

"It will be a long time before you can play then," I say. "All the girls move away from here."

So, off I go and let that strange girl play without me. All day long I have fun. I play on my bike. Then, I build a zoo with blocks for all my animals outside in the yard. And that strange girl does nothing.

At last, I get out some paper and start to draw. I draw and draw for a very long time, and so I forget to look out for the new girl.

Then, in back of me, I hear a small voice say, "Could we be friends?" I turn around and see the new girl.

"Here. Have some paper and a pen," I say to her.

She sits down close to me and says, "I know a song we can sing." It turns out to be a nice song. We sing it over and over. Now the new girl and I are good friends, and she is not strange at all.

Chapter Fifteen

Rhythm At The Zoo

Vocabulary note:

The best approach to this poem would be to read it ahead of time to understand its rhythm. A pause at the end of every line, whether punctuated or not, enables your child to recognize the rhyming words of each verse. However, at the end of verse eight, refrain from breathing until verse nine has begun. I think you will like the effect.

Your child has been introduced to two words with *ing* endings. Those words are *moving* and *swinging*. Pronounce the *ing* sound, and demonstrate how you can add *ing* to the ends of words to create new ones. With words ending in *e*, drop the *e* and add *ing*. Examples are *shaking, having, coming* and *biting*. Some words that end in *t* require adding another *t* before the *ing*, such as: *putting, hitting, letting* and *sitting*. If you are unsure of the *ing* ending, look in the dictionary. The pluralized words in this poem are *monkey, giraffe, elephant, lion, bear, song, tail, shoe* and *open. Th* combination letters are found in the word *their*. *You*, in the ninth verse, should be emphasized. Note the word *till*, condensed from the word *until*. This poem contains two questions.

Vocabulary #15:

am	till	night(s)	their
swinging		monkey(s)	done
stop(s)		line(s)	just
join(s)		giraffe(s)	easy
kick(s)		elephant(s)	strong
		lion(s)	
		bear(s)	
		zebra(s)	
		dance(s)	
		sun	

It is night. I am ready to close up the zoo.

My work is all done. There is nothing to do.

When what do you think I see in the trees?

All of the monkeys are swinging by me.

And down on the ground is a very long line

of all the zoo animals that never could climb.

Giraffes, elephants, lions and bears,

all of the animals go by me there.

They can not see me as I move behind.

A zebra and I are the last in the line.

After a while, I hear a strange thing.

The line stops moving, and all start to sing.

The song is different than songs that I know.

You never know just where that nice song will go.

Then, all animals join up, some with tails in their teeth,

but before I can hide, a zebra turns to me,

And he says in a voice that is just like my own,

"What do *you* think of our animal song?"

I say, " It is nice," and he asks me to dance.

But it's more like a hop when there 's ants in your pants.

And I do not find that it's easy to do,

till I take the time to kick off my shoes.

We dance and we dance and we dance all night long,

till the night goes away and the sun comes up strong.

It' s time to go home and stop all this play,

and so, we shake hands, and I tell them good day.

And when the zoo opens, the boys and girls say,

"Why do the animals always sleep in the day?"

Chapter Sixteen

Itchy Illness

Vocabulary note:

Few children, especially those with siblings, escape the *chicken pox*. Although your child is familiar with the word *chicken*, you will not find the words *chicken pox* in the text. Rather, it will be more interesting to note whether or not your child can recognize the symptoms and supply a name for the disease himself. This story was written to expose him to medical terms.

Spots, ears, calls, shows and *hurts* are the latest plurals. The *sh* combination letters are in the word *show*. When introducing the word *who*, be aware that it is an exception to the *wh* combination letter rule, and teach your child to pronounce *who* as *hoo*, not *woo*. This spelling of the word *too* means *also* or *very*.

Vocabulary #16:

mommy	show(s)	doctor(s)	too	sick
people	itch(es)	fever(s)		hot
who	hurt(s)	spot(s)		cold
	call(s)	ear(s)		even
		body(ies)		
		medicine(s)		
		store(s)		
		nurse(s)		

Mommy gives me some breakfast, but I do not want to eat. I think I am sick. My mommy puts her hand on my head and tells me that I am not hot. I do not have a big fever. Then, she sees small, red spots behind my ears.

She calls the doctor. The doctor says that he will come to our house. He does not want the people who call on him to get sick, too. I am in bed when the doctor shows up. He looks me over. The small, red spots are all over my body now. And they itch. The spots are even inside my mouth. My mouth is red and hot. It hurts. Mommy gives me cold things to drink.

I don't want to read. I don't want to play. All I want to do is sleep, but the itch does not go away.

Mommy knows about some medicine that she can get from the store. She goes to get some when dad comes home. Mommy puts the medicine all over my spots. The spots don't itch now.

In three days, there will be no more new spots. Mommy says that the spots will go away soon after that. My mommy is a very good nurse.

Chapter Seventeen

Sun, Sand and Shells

Vocabulary note:

Not all children are fortunate enough to have seen the ocean. Many of them, however, have experienced the family outing and the interaction of family members when responsibilities are left at home. Hopefully, this story will awaken pleasurable memories of past excursions that you and your child have shared.

The vocabulary list contains two compound words: *today* and *sunburn*. Remember to cover the latter half of the compound word first, to facilitate recognition of it, if necessary. *Going* is the third *ing* word to date. The words *feel, burn, itch, shell* and *line* are pluralized. Note the *es* plural ending on the word *itches*.

Vocabulary #17:

an	daddy	going	until	sand(s)	near	many
		feel(s)		ocean(s)		
		burn(s)		water(s)		
		swim(s)		car(s)		
		bury(ies)		window(s)		
		drive(s)		part(s)		
		hold(s)		lunch(es)		
				umbrella(s)		

We are going to the ocean today. It is a long drive in the car. My sister feels sick until I open a car window for her.

The sand is hot, too hot to walk on. It burns our feet. We have to put on our shoes. But the sand gets into our shoes and hurts our feet.

Mommy and daddy sit close to the water. They set up an umbrella in the sand. We will not get a sunburn if we sit under it.

My sister and I want to swim. Daddy says that he will swim near me. He thinks that the water can pull me out over my head. We swim until mom calls us for lunch.

After lunch, my sister and I look for shells. Many of the shells are white. Daddy tells us to hold a big one up to our ears. We can hear the ocean inside it.

Dad picks a spot where he can bury me in the sand. My head is the only part of my body that is not under the sand. I can not move my body at all. Dad tells mom that I can not get lost now. Mom and dad are happy about that. But I am not happy. My nose itches. I ask dad to hurry and get me out of the sand. Daddy and my sister help me out.

All day long we build lots of things in the sand. We put long lines of shells all over the things we make. And daddy takes us for a swim again.

Mommy calls to us. She wants us to come under the umbrella. We have to get out of the sun before we get a sunburn. I look at my feet. They are red and hot. I know I have a sunburn.

We sit for a while and hear the water hit the sand over and over. It makes me want to go to sleep. The day is done. The sun is going down. We get ready to go home now. But I know we will come back when our sunburn is all gone.

Chapter Eighteen

The Gift Exchange

Vocabulary note:

This story will familiarize your child with words associated with the receipt of packages and the postal service. The U.S. Postal Service will not mail animals, excepting poultry. Hence, our baby cat is delivered by a man, not a mailman. You will note that this story, also, ends in a question to which there is no right or wrong answer. It may interest you to explore the logic of your child's response.

Mailman, mailbox and *something* are the three compound words of the text. The plurals are *brings, starts, needs* and *holes*. *Th* combination letters are found in the word *thank*. There are a few exclamations and questions. The word *present* can be pronounced *prez' nt* or *pri zent'*. Introduce both pronunciations even though the latter one will rarely be used at this age level.

Vocabulary #18:

man	bring(s)	because	door(s)	soon	first
	wait(s)		hole(s)		another
	follow(s)		string(s)		pretty
	must		letter(s)		tiny
	grab(s)		present(s)		
	thank(s)		pet(s)		
	cover(s)		way(s)		
	tape(s)		stamp(s)		
	need(s)		mail		

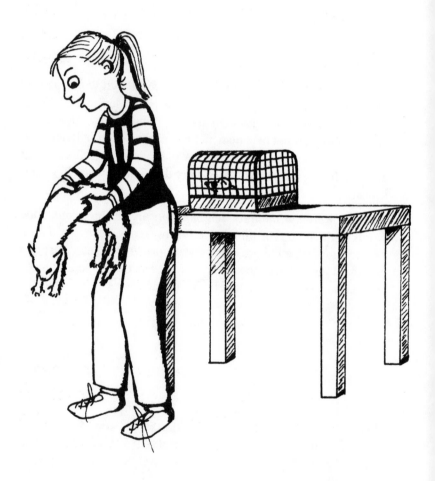

It is my birthday. A man brings a box to my door. The box has holes in it. He says that I have to open the box very soon.

What can it be? I hold the box up and shake it. Something is moving around inside it. I pull off the string and open the first box. There is another box inside. It has pretty paper all over it, but the paper has holes in it, too.

There is a letter. It is from grandma and grandpa. They can not wait to hear if I like their present.

I take the pretty paper off the box and open it. Inside there is a tiny baby cat. She jumps out and starts to walk all over the house. What a nice present!

I follow her and see her climb the stairs and go into my room. She must smell my pet mouse, because she is there near it. She will grab my mouse if I don't hurry. My new baby cat only sees that mouse one time, but she does not forget. I find her at my door all the time.

What can I do? I know! I will give my

mouse away to grandma and grandpa. It will be a nice way to say thank you.

I put my mouse in a box and cover it with pretty paper. There are holes in this box, too. Then I cover the outside box with brown paper and tape it. I put a string all around it. Now, I need to write their names on the box. My thank you letter to grandma and grandpa needs a stamp, too. After I find a stamp, I will mail my letter in our mailbox outside. The mailman will pick it up soon.

I can not give my mouse to the mailman to mail. He will not take it. Another man must bring the mouse to grandma's house.

Boy, I can not wait until grandma and grandpa get my present! Do you think they will like it?

Chapter Nineteen

From Pen To Pen At The Farm

Vocabulary note:

One of the highlights of the school year, beginning with nursery school, is the class trip. A visit to a farm was chosen as the theme for this story because of the fascination that children possess for animals, especially baby animals.

In the text you will find the compound word *piglets*. The plurals are *works, climbs, cows, horses, pigs, hens, chicks, legs, falls, eggs, waits* and *joins*. Note the *ch* letter combination in the word *chick*. The story concludes with a question and its furnished answer.

Vocabulary #19:

woman	meet(s)	trip(s)	no	old
	stay(s)	farm(s)		wet
	try(ies)	barn(s)		next
	push(es)	farmer(s)		little
	fall(s)	cow(s)		noisy
		horse(s)		
		pig(s)		
		hen(s)		
		chick(s)		
		leg(s)		
		fence(s)		
		grass(es)		

The boys and girls from my school are going on a trip to a farm. An old woman comes out of a barn to meet us. She will show us the farm while the farmer works. They have cows, horses, pigs and hens.

The chicks always stay close to the hen's legs. They know she is big and strong. No one will hurt them. One of the hen's eggs is not open. She waits for her chick. We look at the egg, too, and see the shell start to break. The baby chick comes out of his egg. He is all wet. The baby joins the mommy hen in the yard.

Next, we go to see the pig. She has a lot of little piglets. They try to drink milk from their mommy at the same time. They push and push and push. I think they could all drink if only they could wait for it. The old woman starts to walk away, but one of the boys climbs up on the fence to show off. He falls down next to the pigs. And when they pull him out, he is all brown and wet. He gets even more wet when the old woman makes him wash all of his body and clothes in water. He looks good, but he smells like a pig.

We are ready to see the cows and horses now. They eat grass behind a fence. No cows or horses want to come close to us. We must be too noisy. Their tails are always swinging. That makes the flies stay away from them.

We have to get back to school, and the old woman has to help the farmer with his work. We thank the woman and get in our cars. It is a very hot day. I don't have a nice drive home. Why not? I have to sit next to the boy who smells like a pig.

Chapter Twenty

The Airshow

Vocabulary note:

This is our longest story to date. In reviewing the preceding stories and poems, you will observe that many of the sentences have become more complex. Instead of saying, "The boy comes home from school. The girl asks the boy to go to the store for her," the sentence would be reworded to say, "When the boy comes home from school, the girl asks him to go to the store for her." Creating more interesting sentences requires the employment of such grammatical tools as the prepositional phrase and the adverbial clause. An example of a prepositional phrase is-" Regarding your homework, I think you could do a better job." Whereas, adverbial clauses sound like this- " After the game was over, we all drove to my house." It is unnecessary to shield your child from complicated sentence structures. His comprehension will not suffer, and the exposure to these sentences will encourage him to express his ideas creatively.

Stand, car, ticket, plane, radio, head, pull, color, parachute, hang and *way* are pluralized. Contained in this story are the compound words, *airshow, airplane, something* and *tonight*. Note all questions and exclamations.

Vocabulary #20:

stand(s)	above	street(s)	how	slow
carry(ies)	across	airport(s)		much
buy(s)	toward	middle		faster
keep(s)		air		four
		ticket(s)		right
		money		
		plane(s)		
		radio(s)		
		parachute(s)		
		color(s)		
		top(s)		

Across the street from my house, there is an airport. Today, when I am done with breakfast, I look out the window. There are two long lines of cars in the street. A man stands in the middle of them and lets the cars turn into the airport. I ask my dad to tell me what is going on. He says that today is the day of the airshow.

Dad asks me to go to the show with him. We make a lunch to bring with us. Daddy will carry it on his back. He takes my hand as we walk around all the slow-moving cars.

Here is where we buy the tickets. Daddy asks the man to tell him how much the tickets are. When the man gives my daddy some of the money back, daddy lets me keep it. He wants me to buy something fun with the money.

The show is not ready to start. We walk around the airport and look at all the planes that are on the ground. One of the planes is so big that it can carry many, many cars inside it. We can walk into this airplane. I am so tiny. How could people build this big plane?

There is a show over by a fence. Some people fly their toy airplanes with radios that they hold in their hands.

It gets noisy now. Some airplanes are ready to start. We hear a man's voice tell us that we will see people jump from the airplanes. Then, way above our heads, we see many black spots behind an airplane. The spots are people. They fall faster and faster. I do not like this. What if they hit the ground? But wait! What is this? The people have put their hands and feet out. They look like birds. It is a slow fall now. One man flies over to another man and they hold hands. Then, the two of them fly over to another man. The three of them hold hands. It must be time for them to get ready to drop to the ground. The man in the middle pulls something. A parachute opens out in back of him. It pulls him up and away. Soon we see all the pretty colors of the parachutes as they open up. One by one, they drop to the ground and are safe.

Next, we see a woman on top of an airplane. A man sits inside the plane, but the woman is on the outside. He will fly the plane while she stands on top of it. The plane takes off. The woman's long, brown hair flies in back of her. Some boys near us say that it must be easy to stand there. They say the woman can not move. Then the plane starts to turn over. The woman is under the plane, and her hair hangs toward the ground. The boys will not make fun of her again!

It is time to see something new. Four planes fly over us. They fly very close to one another. When one plane turns, all the planes turn. When one plane climbs high in the air, all the planes climb after him. Now all four planes go different ways. Two of the planes turn around and fly right at one another. Just as they are about to hit, one plane turns over on his back, and they go by one another. They are safe for now.

My daddy and I are happy that we have come to the airshow today. Our lunch was very good, and daddy let me buy a toy plane that we can try to fly around the yard. I know when I go to bed tonight, I will not sleep. I will think about the day that I learn to fly an airplane. That is what I want to do when I am big.

Chapter Twenty-One

Impressions Of The City

Vocabulary note:

Your child has reached the final *story* of this course. Turn to the next chapter, however, before informing him that he is all done.

Do you realize the amount of material he has absorbed? You will have experienced the thrill of watching your child's interest and abilities snowball, providing that you have refrained from pressuring him into learning. Chances are good that he is taking the initiative to read anything that is available to him. As I said in the beginning of this book, there is genuine satisfaction for the parent who is instrumental in opening his child's eyes to a world beyond that child's imagination. For all the world's knowledge is written down, and the child, who can read well, has access to that kaleidoscope of ideas and experiences. So, mom and dad enjoy! It is time for you and your child to visit the big city before we close these story pages.

The plurals in the text are *follows, farms, stores, slows, helps, stops, grabs, sells, buys, buildings, meets, draws* and *surprises*. Note the two exclamations.

Vocabulary #21:

been	city(ies)	almost	still
took	train(s)		loud
tired	river(s)		any
sell(s)	subway(s)		tall
enjoy	food		
did	cart(s)		
	building(s)		
	place(s)		

Grandma and grandpa want to take me into the city with them. My daddy works in the city. We will meet him for lunch.

Grandma and grandpa are too old to drive a car. We must take a train into the city. I have never been on a train before. A man walks toward us and asks grandpa for our tickets. Grandma is not very happy with me, because I can not sit still. They let me sit next to the window. There is so much to see! The train follows a river for a lot of the trip. At first, there are farms, with cows and horses, to see. Then, there are more and more houses and stores, until I can not see many trees or much grass at all. The train slows down. It is time for us to get off the train. The man who took our tickets helps me and grandma off. He is a nice man.

Grandpa says we have to find the subway. The subway looks like a train. But I think it is much faster. Grandma gets to sit down. I have to stand in the middle and hold on to grandpa's leg. When the subway train stops, I almost fall down, but grandpa grabs my coat.   The subway is under the ground, and we have to climb many stairs before we see the sun again.

It is noisy outside. There are cars and people all over.   It is not this loud at home. Grandma and I are tired after our climb. We need some food.   A man sells hot dogs from a cart on the street under a big umbrella. We buy three hot dogs.

Now, grandma wants to buy some things for her house. We stop in store after store after store. I do not enjoy this part of our trip.   We don't see any toys, and grandma is so very slow. I try to be good, but I think I will run around soon if she does not hurry. I am just about to pull my hand away from grandpa's when grandma sees a toy store. That is more like it! We go inside, and she buys me a furry bear.

It is time to meet my daddy now. He works in one of the tall buildings down the street. Daddy meets us near the door. I give him a hug and show him my bear. There is a nice place to eat across the street. It is always fun to have lunch with daddy. He draws pictures on the paper napkins.

After lunch, daddy has to go back to work. Grandma and grandpa take me to see a show. It is a show for little people like me. I know grandpa did not like it much, but I did. I still have the tickets.

It has been a long day. I am tired. I think I will sleep all the way home. I thank grandma and grandpa. Grandma looks so happy when I say thank you. I don't always like where my grandma and grandpa take me. But I always thank them, and I am always good. Then they ask me to come with them again and again, and grandma and grandpa like to give me many, different surprises.

Chapter Twenty-Two

Reading As A Way Of Life

Vocabulary note:

Are you surprised to encounter another vocabulary list? The purpose of this list is to permit your child to read the following letter that is addressed to either him or her. While attempting to demonstrate to him that reading is not limited to stories and poems, I have also included a recipe and page of jokes that are easily understood at this age level. Regarding the recipe, no mention has been made of the use of potholders or of oven temperature. Four and five year olds do not have the strength necessary to carry a pan of chicken, much less put it in the oven. Consequently, parental assistance is required. Set the oven at four-hundred degrees and allow the chicken to cook between a half an hour and an hour depending on the cut you buy.

Your child has been supplied with all the tools necessary to become an independent reader. Although the chapter contains a vocabulary list and instructions for parents, refering to compound words, plurals, *ing* endings, etc., I suspect that your child's own abilities deletes the necessity for them, relegating the preparatory work to mere routine.

Hopefully, you are keeping your child well immersed in books from the library. If you discover a lengthy book that you know he will enjoy, you may want to consider sharing the reading with him, he reads one page and you read the next, so that he does not become overtired. One advantage to reading side by side is that you can help pronounce and define unfamiliar words for your child.

Once it is evident that your child has become a voracious reader, consider introducing him to the nonfiction section of your library. Ask the librarian for a list enumerating the subject groups of the Dewey Decimal System. Each set of one-hundred numbers will be classified under a broad subject heading. For example, the 500s are grouped under the title, Science. However, within that set of books, you will see publications on a variety of topics- plants, animals, dinosaurs, the weather, astronomy, mathematics, etc. Lead your child through each subject group in order, and as you skim the spine of each book, read aloud the titles that you think will be of interest to your child. Feel free to pull books from the shelves for closer inspection. Nonfiction books cater to all ages. Allow your child the joy of choosing for himself. You may be tempted to interfere when he chooses some books that are obviously too mature for him, but experience should teach him to recognize those books that will bore him with their difficult content. If he is unable to make this adjustment, then it is time for you to become his guide.

You have probably wondered what you are going to do if there is no outlet for your child's reading abilities when he enters kindergarten. I suggest that you inform his teacher that he can read and ask what the teacher is willing to do about it. Schools,with adequate parental pressure, sometimes establish kindergarten reading groups for those who can and can not read. You can encourage your child to read everything in the classroom, and inquire whether he could read a story to his class on a regular basis. Remember though, encouragement at home is a necessity. His reading ability should not be regulated by his grade level at school but rather, his interest in life.

In the letter to a boy, your child will discover the compound words *ago, everyday, anything, somewhere* and *storywriter*. The words *learn* and *read* have *ing* endings. There should be no problem with the *r* and *er* endings of *storywriter* and *reader*. Plurals found in the letter are *boxes, windows* and *jokes*. Notice all punctuation.

The letter written to a girl introduces the word *live* which can be pronounced two different ways. Be sure to discuss both pro-nunciations, because the knowledge will be needed in this chapter. Compound words of this letter are *everyone, everywhere, every-day, schoolroom, something* and *storywriter*. The words *learn* and *tell* have *ing* endings. Note the *r* and *er* endings of *storywriter* and *reader*. *Live, use, recipe, joke, place, street, cook* and *jar* are pluralized. Questions and exclamations pepper the page.

Compound words of the recipe are *anymore, tablespoons* and *something*. The only new plural is the word *bones.*

Finally, our observations of the joke page are as follows. The word *tear* can be pronounced *teer* or *tare.* Compound words were essential to the punch line of many of the jokes. They are *armchair, seahorse, catfish, bellybutton, barnyard, schoolroom, bookworm* and *waterfall.* Your child is familiar with the word *cover* and will now be exposed to *covered.* Sounding the word out will assist his recognition of it. The pluralized words are *hold, tear, part* and *dog.*

Vocabulary #22:

bubble(s)	button(s)	together	other
stir(s)	salt		every
live(s)	pan(s)		
use(s)	butter(s)		
	flour(s)		
	oven(s)		
	octopus(es)		
	arm(s)		
	sea(s)		
	belly(ies)		
	tear(s)		
	recipe(s)		
	joke(s)		

To the big boy who can read,

You have come a long way. Now you are a good reader, and you could not read at all a while ago. You must be very happy! Everyday you will see more and more words. And when you are old, you will still be learning new words. You can read many books because of all the words you know.

It is lots of fun to learn about different things all the time. If you want to know about animals in the ocean, you can pick up a book and read about them. If you want to learn about anything, there is a book somewhere that you can read.

Look around you. Do you see the words on the food boxes that were left on the table after breakfast? Can you read the words that are all over the windows of the stores you go by? And when you go to school, look around the room, and you will see many things to read.

If you want to cook, you will have to read the recipe. If you want to tell jokes, you can find them in a book. There are some jokes in this book for you to tell your family and friends after you are done reading this letter. And you can ask your mom or dad if they will let you try the recipe that is at the back of this book, with their help.

Have fun, little one!

Your friend,
the storywriter

To the big girl who can read,

Look at all the work you have done
and what a good reader you are! Don't you
think it is fun to sit down with a book and
learn about the lives of other people and
their animals? Do you like to read about
places you have never been to? Not
everyone is like you. So, it is nice to meet
them all.

You can find words all over the
place. Look out the window when your
mom and dad take you for a drive in the car.
What do you see? There are words on the
stores, words on the streets, even words on
the cars. When your mommy cooks dinner,
do you see the words all over the jars that
she uses? You will even find words
everywhere in your schoolroom when it is
time for you to go there.

You will learn new words everyday.
Even your mommy and daddy are still
learning new words. The more words you

know, the more books you can read.

Books are not the only things you can read. You can read recipes, if you want to cook something, or you can read jokes to tell to the people you know. After you read this letter, look in the back of the book. You will find a recipe there, and you can ask your mom or dad if they will let you try it with their help. Look some more. Do you see the jokes? Have fun telling the jokes to your family!

Your friend,
the storywriter

A Recipe for Chicken on Toast

(for dinner or lunch)

1. Wash the chicken.

2. Put the chicken in a pan.

3. Place the pan in a hot oven.

4. Cook the chicken in the oven until it is done.

5. When the chicken is not hot anymore, pick the meat off the bones in little bits, and put the chicken bits in a bowl.

6. Make toast for all the people who are going to eat.

7. Put four tablespoons of butter in a pan and cook it. When it is done, it will bubble and look like something you could drink, not something that you eat. Don't burn the butter.

8. Then, put four tablespoons of flour into the butter and stir the two together until they bubble.

9. Put two cups of milk into the pan, and after the milk starts to bubble, stir it for a little while.

10. Drop the bits of chicken into the pan, and stir them to make the chicken hot again.

11. Shake salt and pepper into the pan.

12. Spoon the hot food that is in the pan on top of the toast.

JOKES

Where does an octopus sit?

in an armchair

What animal never wears clothes?

a bear

What farm animal lives in the ocean?

a seahorse

Where do monkeys live?

in tree houses

What part of your clothes could hurt you?

your socks

What fish does not like dogs?

the catfish

What part of your body holds all the other parts together?

your bellybutton

What do you find in a barnyard and a schoolroom?

pens

Who always reads while he eats?

a bookworm

What is another name for tears?

a waterfall

How are four eggs like the sand by the sea?

they are covered with shells